UNIFORMS ILLUSTRATED No 7

Cover illustration: German infantry wearing special padded winter uniforms, white side outermost; Eastern Front, 1943.

1. A German corporal bringing food up to front-line troops – a hazardous job which required a soldier to cross open ground with a heavy metal container strapped to his back and to be exposed to enemy fire when approaching outlying German-held positions.

UNIFORMS ILLUSTRATED NO. 7

German Combat Uniforms of World War Two

Volume II

BRIAN L. DAVIS

ARMS AND ARMOUR PRESS
London – Melbourne – Harrisburg, Pa. – Cape Town

Uniforms Illustrated 7: German Combat Uniforms of World War Two, Vol. II
Published in 1985 by Arms and Armour Press, Lionel Leventhal Limited, 2–6 Hampstead High Street, London NW3 1QQ; 11 Munro Street, Port Melbourne 3207, Australia; Sanso Centre, 8 Adderley Street, P.O. Box 94, Cape Town 8000; Cameron and Kelker Streets, P.O. Box 1831, Harrisburg, Pennsylvania 17105, USA

British Library Cataloguing in Publication Data:
Davis, Brian L.
German combat uniforms of World War Two.—
(Uniforms illustrated; 7)
Vol. 2
1. Germany, *Wehrmacht*—Uniforms—Pictorial works
I. Title II. Series
355.1'4'0943 UC485.G3
ISBN 0-85368-666-1

Edited and laid out by Roger Chesneau.
Printed in Italy
by Tipolitografia G. Canale & C. S.p.A. - Turin
in association with Keats European Ltd.

Introduction

When German ground forces went to war on 1 September 1939 all the troops were clothed according to the requirements for field service. The early campaigns were all contained within the borders of Europe, and there was little time – or need – for improvement to or improvisation of uniform clothing. However, the war in North Africa and the first harsh winter after the invasion of the Soviet Union in the summer of 1941 brought about the need for new forms and styles of uniforms and clothing garments. Camouflage clothing, for example, initially used on a limited scale and then in the main by units of the Waffen-SS (Armed-SS), very rapidly became commonplace. The need for concealment became more acute as the war progressed and especially as the Allies gradually obtained mastery of the skies over Europe.

The raw materials needed for the manufacture of uniforms became increasingly in short supply, resulting in a decline in the quality of the cloth used – which in turn had a direct effect on the appearance of the uniform. Many items of clothing that did not exist in 1939 came into widespread use during the later part of the war. These can be divided roughly into two types – those produced officially and issued to the troops and those manufactured out of necessity and which, although worn universally by the armed forces, did not constitute official uniform garments. Both these categories can be seen in the specially selected photographs featured in this book.

Brian L. Davis

◀ 2

2. Tough, battle-hardened German combat soldiers were nicknamed collectively (and affectionately) 'Front Schwein' – front-line swine. Like combat soldiers the world over, their lifestyle when in action was dangerous, dirty and uncomfortable. A pause during house-to-house street fighting allows this Grenadier time for a short rest. He is particularly laden, with rucksack, helmet, greatcoat and full equipment.

▲3

▲4 ▼5

3. A three-man machine gun crew. One fires the weapon, another feeds ammunition into the gun and observes the shoot (and, in this picture, uses a field telephone, presumably passing back information to rear-area troops) and the third man supports the machine gun and helps bring up extra ammunition.
4. Two shots, one kill. An ecstatic 88mm gun crew firing over level sights have destroyed an enemy tank with their second round.
5. German assault troops (Stosstruppen) fighting for the city of Leningrad pour fire into Russian positions.
6, 7. Two photographs taken in sequence showing German infantry probing towards enemy positions, the latter just discernible as protected dugouts. Photograph 6 shows three soldiers protected by covering fire from a machine gun (far left) about to throw their stick grenades; photo 7 shows the men, prone, watching the resulting explosions.

6▲ 7▼

▲8
8. A light mortar about to be fired by a two-man crew somewhere in Italy.

9▶
9. A soldier from a Mountain Troop Regiment aims his machine gun. The weapon is mounted on a heavy tripod for use against aircraft.

▲10

10. Stripped to the waist, two men from a Smoke Troop Unit load explosive projectiles into their multi-barrelled mortar.
11. An anti-tank gun in action on the Italian Adriatic Front.
12. A red hot flame-thrower nozzle provides a soldier with a light for his cigarette.
13. German troops observe the enemy from the shelter of a bomb crater while a comrade snatches a short rest.
14. Hands thrust deep into the pockets of his greatcoat, and with his coat collar turned up against the cold wind, a sentry peers skywards while manning his heavy, tripod-mounted, anti-aircraft machine gun.
15. Fusiliers from the 'Grossdeutschland' Division clear the remains of a burnt-out house somewhere on the Eastern Front.

▼11

12▲ 13▼

14▲ 15▼

▲16

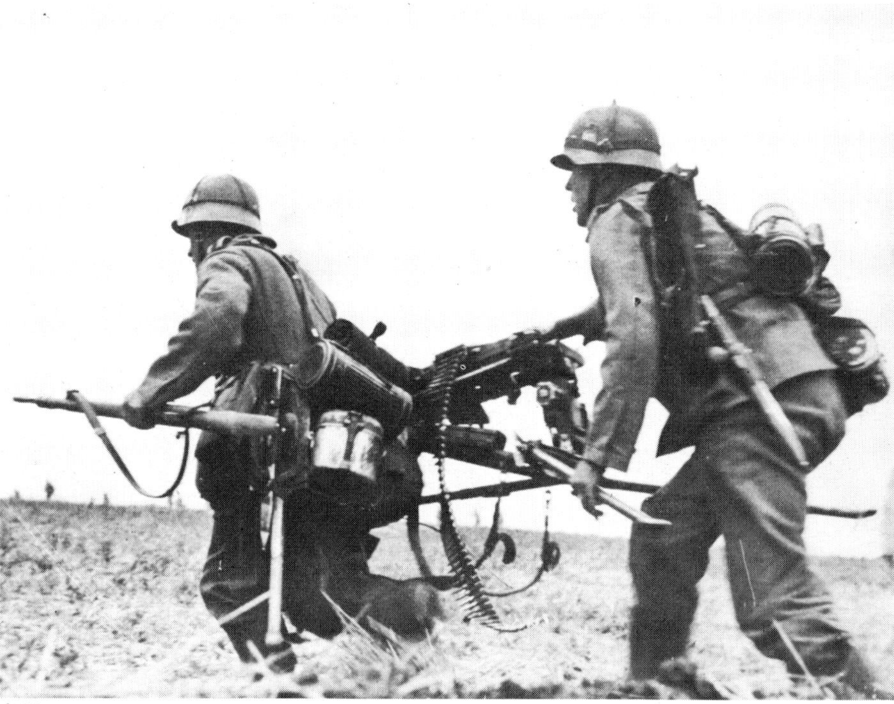

▲17

16. German Infantry fighting around the city of Sebastopol take cover after coming under fire from a Russian machine gun.
17. At the run, a two-man team carries a heavy, tripod-mounted machine gun to its next firing position. Although both men are fully equipped, the rear soldier is carrying an extra gas mask cylinder and gas plan bag.

18. Two NCOs, both armed with sub-machine guns, take cover behind an earth bank during the early fighting for the Russian city of Stalingrad.
19. A 'Spandau' machine gun supported by at least five riflemen awaits the advance of the enemy in a field of vegetables.

18▼

19▼

◀20 21▲ 22▼

20. Heavy and continuous fighting on the Eastern Front (and on other fronts for that matter) rapidly reduced the ordinary foot soldier to a scruffy individual, wearing and carrying only those items that were absolutely necessary for his task and for his survival.
21. Young soldiers from a Luftwaffe Field Division in conversation. All wear camouflage clothing. The soldier on the right has a cloth camouflage cover over his steel helmet whilst the soldier to the left is wearing a mosquito net rolled up over his helmet and tied in position.
22. A member of the Field Police directs a Tiger tank to the front.

▲23

24▶

23. With the coming of the spring weather on the Eastern Front, it was necessary to abandon every vestige of snow camouflage and revert to dull field grey, a colour more suitable to the green and brown of the trees and earth. The photograph shows a soldier re-painting his steel helmet.

24. As discussed in *Uniforms Illustrated 5*, companion volume to the present work, all the items illustrated in the colour plates were worn on the German Army Field Service uniform, and the reader is again referred to the author's *German Army Uniforms and Insignia, 1933–1945* for further details.

A. Cuff-title for personnel of Infantry Regiment 'Grossdeutschland' (Greater Germany); worn on right forearm.
B. Shoulder strap for a Generalleutnant.
C. Collar patch (right side) for a Generalfeldmarschall.
D. Motor Vehicle Driver's Badge of Merit in silver; worn on left forearm.
E. Shoulder strap worn by Other Ranks personnel of Smoke Troop units.
F. Shoulder strap for an Unteroffizier of the Deutsches Afrika Korps, Mountain Troop Unit.
G. Gebirgsjäger BeVo quality arm badge; worn on right upper arm.
H. Arm band for personnel, either civilian or paramilitary, attached to the German Armed Forces; worn on upper left arm.
I. Collar patch (right side) for Other Ranks personnel of Infantry units.
J, K. Two (pair of) Special Badges for the single-handed destruction of an enemy tank, silver grade; worn on upper left arm.
L. Shoulder strap for a Leutnant in Grenadier-Regiment 134 (Hoch und Deutschmeister).
M. Shoulder strap for a Stabsfeldwebel from a Panzer-Grenadier Regiment.
N, O, P. Trade badges for a Waffenfeldwebel (Ordnance NCO); all worn on right forearm.
Q, R. Trade badge for a Gerätverwaltungs Unteroffizier (Supply Administration NCO); worn on right forearm.
S. Cuff-title worn by German personnel of the Deutsches Afrika Korps; worn on right forearm.

A
B
C
D
E
F
G
Im Dienst
der
DeutschenWehrmach
H
I
J
K
L
M
N
O
P
Q
R
AFRIKAKORPS
S

A
B
C
D
E
601
F
G
H
I
J
K
L
M
N
O
P
KUBAN
Q
R
S
Propagandakompanie

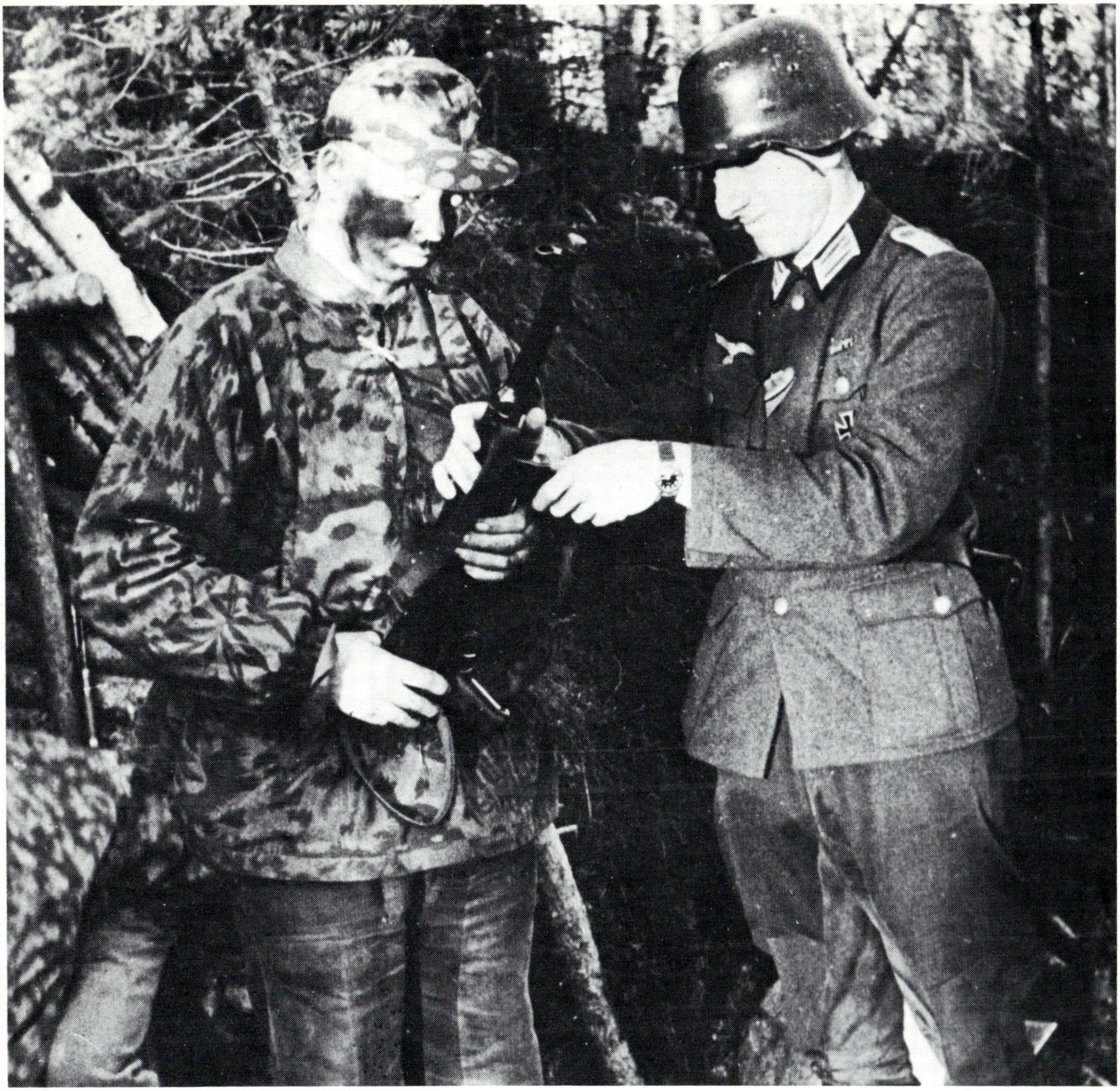

◀25 26▲

25. **A.** Cuff-title for personnel of Infantry Regiment 271 'Feldherrnhalle'; worn on left forearm.
B. Rank badge for an Oberschütze; worn on upper left arm.
C. Rank chevron for a Gefreiter; worn on upper left arm.
D. Rank chevrons for an Obergefreiter with less than six years service; worn on upper left arm.
E. Rank chevrons for an Obergefreiter with more than six years service; worn on upper left arm. Items B to E inclusive were rank insignia in use from 1942 to 1945.
F. Shoulder strap for a Funker (Signaller) from Signals Regiment 601.
G. German Army National Emblem (Breast Eagle), BeVo quality.
H. Shoulder strap for an Oberfeldwebel from an Army Anti-Aircraft (Flak) Unit.
I. Shoulder strap for a soldier from an armoured unit or anti-tank unit serving with the DAK (Deutsches Afrika Korps).
J. Shoulder strap for a Funker (Signaller) from Infantry Regiment 'Grossdeutschland'.
K. Trade badge for an Engineer (Pioneer) Unit Signals Operator; worn on upper left sleeve.
L. Trade badge for an Infantry Unit Signals Operator; worn on upper left arm.
M. Trade badge for a Panzer Unit Signals Operator; worn on upper left arm.
N. Trade badge for a Signals Operator from a Rifle or Mountain Troop Regiment; worn on upper left arm.
O. Rank badge for an Oberschütze from an Armoured (Panzer) unit; worn on left upper arm. See also item B above.
P. Arm band for a war blinded military person; worn on left upper arm.
Q. Campaign arm shield for troops who were engaged in the Kuban fighting; worn on upper left arm.
R. Collar patch (left side) for general wear by Other Ranks of different branches of service, late war issue.
S. Cuff-title for personnel of the ranks of the Army Propaganda Corps; worn on both left and right forearms at different times.

26. The German Army employed two patterns of camouflage for various items of clothing and the Waffen-SS at least five distinctive patterns and two basic colour schemes. The patterns used by the Army were quite different from those used by the Waffen-SS and usually there was no intermixing of patterns between the two branches of the Wehrmacht. However, in this interesting photograph a soldier from an Assault Troop operating on the Karelian Front in Finland is shown wearing a Waffen-SS summer-pattern camouflage smock and field cap.

▲27 ▼28

29▶

27. Men of an Infantry Company with their officer (centre) trudge wearily across the Russian steppes.
28. German Infantry move up from a river crossing, August 1943.
29. Infantry on the march pause for a short rest and a welcome smoke.

◀30

31▲

30. Soldiers quench their thirst with water trickling from a primitive wooden viaduct.

31. Large rubber, inflatable dinghies like this were used as floating pontoons for bridge building and for transporting troops during river-crossing operations – and also for more leisurely tasks. Here, supplies of bread are delivered somewhere in a safe area.

32. A four-man rubber dinghy is hauled out from the safety of a trench ready for a river patrol by men from a reconnaissance unit.

32▼

▲33 ▼34

▼35

36▲

33. German Infantry clamber out from the comparative safety of a ditch during the fighting around the Crimean city of Sebastopol.
34. German troops take it easy around a haystack somewhere on the Eastern Front.
35. A German sentry watches over a frozen river somewhere in East Prussia.
36. Troops fighting in the area around the French city of Caen pause for a smoke. They are wearing camouflage uniforms, complete with camouflage helmet covers.
37. Members of a Pioneer Unit serving in North Africa as part of the Deutsches Afrika Korps watch intently as a soft-skinned, four-wheeled truck is gingerly moved along a temporary wooden bridge built across a deep anti-tank ditch excavated by the British while defending the area around Tobruk.

37▼

38. Special leather cases were essential items of equipment for those soldiers who had to use or carry maps. Such a map case is worn here by the motorcyclist in the foreground.
39. From the protection of a slit trench, a German officer waves his men on to their next position. Although his appearance is similar to the ordinary soldiers around him, the officer is wearing leather gloves, carries a map case slung by a strap over his right shoulder and has a pair of field glasses hung around his neck. He carries his personal weapon, a Luger, in a leather holster on his waist-belt.

◀38

39▼

40. Essential Field Service equipment as used on active duty. An 'A' frame is attached to the 'Y' straps and to the former is strapped a loaf of bread, a water bottle, and a rolled shelter quarter. Below this hangs the gas mask container, whilst attached to the waist-belt are the bread bag and water bottle with drinking cup. An extra belt of ammunition is carried around the neck, and the soldier is also equipped with a bayonet in its scabbard.
41. German troops in shirt-sleeve order and still wearing their lifebelts disembark from a vessel somewhere in the Greek Islands.
42. German Infantry wearing full battle order wait their turn to be ferried across a river somewhere on the Eastern Front.
◀40

41▲ 42▼

▲43 ▼44

▲45 ▼46

47▲ 48▼

43. Somewhat dishevelled, these Grenadiers wait under cover before moving forward during a series of battles that took place between the Rivers Donez and Don.
44. A German Infantry foot patrol picks its way through wreckage during the early stages of the fighting for Stalingrad.
45. General of Infantry Wöhler, the Commander of an Army Group and holder of the Knights Cross, makes a tour of inspection in company with senior Rumanian Army officers of an Army Weapons School.
46. A detachment of potential NCOs parades in tropical uniform in the North African desert, February 1942.
47. A two-man machine-gun team. The gunner operates and fires the gun as the number two feeds the belt of ammunition from the ammunition box into the breech of the weapon.
48. A young Mountain Troop officer receives instruction from another officer.

▲49

49. The view from the turret of a German tank. The commander of the tank, wearing earphones, surveys the effect of incendiary rounds fired at enemy positions.
50. A member of the Waffen-SS, heavily clad in an animal-skin, fleece-lined overcoat, talks to the driver of a Russian locomotive.
51. An Army motorcycle rider cautiously inches his machine across a freshly repaired crater, a mixed unit of German troops operating on the Dalmatian coast having been brought up to the scene of this act of sabotage carried out by Yugoslav partisans. Despite the warm weather, which has allowed the repair party to be dressed in lightweight tropical uniforms, it is still necessary for the despatch rider to wear the special protective motorcycle coat.
52. A German Army spotter aircraft, the famous Fieseler Storch, flies alongside a column of military vehicles. This photograph was taken in May 1942 and the crude form of disruptive camouflage still adorns the vehicles from the previous winter: compare this effort at snow camouflage with the all-white painted vehicles and weapons used by the Germans during the succeeding winters on the Eastern Front. The soldier facing the camera is wearing the extra thick winter greatcoat introduced during the war.

50▶

51▲ 52▼

▲53

54▶

53. In muddy conditions on the Eastern Front, full use was made of the Kettenkrad by those units fortunate enough to have them on strength. This vehicle, which was a cross between a motorcycle and a tracked vehicle, was capable of carrying small loads of stores, ammunition and the like or of transporting two men in addition to the driver; it could also tow a small trailer.

54. A, B. Trade badges for a qualified farrier; worn on right forearm.
C, D, E. Trade badges for a Feuerwerker (NCO artificer or ordnance technician); worn on right forearm.
F. Shoulder strap for an Unteroffizier from an armoured reconnaissance unit.
G. Shoulder strap for a Hauptmann from Motor-Cycle Unit from Infantry Regiment 'Grossdeutschland'.
H. Shoulder strap for Other Ranks of a Transport Unit.
I. Shoulder strap for Unteroffizier on the staff of a recruiting office in Military District (Wehrkreis) XVIII (Styria, Carinthia, Tyrol and Slovenia; headquarters at Salzburg).
J. Shoulder strap for a Kanonier (gunner) from the 6th Artillery Observation Regiment.
K. Shoulder strap for an Administrative Branch Pharmaceutical Leutnant.
L. Field Service collar patch (right side) for an Administrative Paymaster Official.
M. Field Service collar patch (right side) for an Administrative District Official.
N. Field Service collar patch (right side) for a Remount Official.
O. Field Service collar patch (right side) for a Medical Officer.
P. Field Service collar patch (right side) for a Pioneer (Engineer) Officer.
Q. Collar patch (right side) for an Army Chaplain.
R. Arm Eagle emblem for Other Ranks and NCOs of Field Police Units (Feldgendarmerie); worn on upper left arm.
S. Special rank insignia for an Unteroffizier.
T. Special rank insignia for a Feldwebel. Items S and T were used on German Army (and Waffen-SS) camouflage and special combat clothing only, on upper left arm.
U. Arm badge for qualified helmsman of engineer assault boats; worn on left upper arm.
V. Arm badge for former member of the Technical Emergency Corps (TeNo) serving in the Army; worn on upper right arm.
W. Cuff-title worn by Army and Luftwaffe Guard Personnel at the Führer's Headquarters; worn on left forearm.

A
B
C
D
E
F
G
H
I
J
K
L
M
N
O
P
Q
R
S
U
V
T
W

A
Stabshelferin des Heeres
B
C
D
E
F
G
10
XII
H
I
J
K
L
M
4
N
O
P
Q
R
S
17
T
Stabshelferin des Heeres

55. A. Cuff-title for a senior female staff assistant in the German Army.
B. Shoulder strap for a Major of Smoke Troops.
C. Shoulder strap for a Pioneer (Engineer) Soldier.
D. Shoulder strap for an Oberfeldwebel from Infantry Regiment 10.
E. Shoulder strap for an Oberfeldwebel from a recruiting office in Military District XII (Eifel, part of Hesse, the Palatinate and Saar area, Lorraine including the Nancy area, and the Grand Duchy of Luxembourg; headquarters at Wiesbaden).
F. Shoulder strap for an Infantry Unteroffizier. The yellow tab is an inter-regimental device.
G. Shoulder strap for an Oberstleutnant concerned with weapons systems.
H. Shoulder strap for a Leutnant on the staff of an Army Gas School or a Smoke Troop School.
I. Shoulder strap for a Leutnant on the staff of an Artillery Observation Training Regiment.
J. Shoulder strap for a Hauptmann (Captain) of Supply Troops.
K. Shoulder strap for an Oberintendanturrat.
L. Shoulder strap for an Oberstleutnant of Mountain Troops.
M. Shoulder strap for an Assistanzarzt.
N. Shoulder strap for an Oberstleutnant from Infantry Regiment 'Grossdeutschland'.
O. Shoulder strap for an Unterwachtmeister from Cavalry Regiment 17.
P. Shoulder strap for an Unteroffizier from an Artillery or an Assault Artillery Unit.
Q. Shoulder strap for a Musician at the Army School of Music.
R. Shoulder strap for a soldier from a Motorized Reconnaissance Unit.
S. Shoulder strap for a Captain of Field Police.
T. Cuff-title for a female staff assistant in the German Army.
56. A heavy tank drives out of a muddy waterhole somewhere to the north-east of Bielgorod.

◀**55**

56▼

▲57 ▼58

59▶

57. Despite their somewhat incongruous appearance, the fur-lined caps worn by these German gunners afforded far better protection to the wearers' heads than was the case with the field caps worn by the other troops shown in this photograph. The idea for these fur caps was probably copied from the Russian troops – indeed, many would have been captured items. They were normally worn with the ear and neck flaps turned up.

58. Sand was occasionally encountered in the Eastern territories as well as in the North African theatre and could prove very troublesome. The photograph shows a convoy held up because the leading vehicles are trapped in soft sand. Troops aided by brushwood placed under the wheels to give purchase help push the vehicle forward and thus get the convoy on the move once again.

59. A mud-caked motorcycle combination and rider. German military motorcycles were manufactured without mudguards or windshields, and it was therefore necessary that some form of basic protection be available to the riders of these machines – hence the issue of special rubberized motorcycle coats.

▲60

▲61 ▼62

60. For a member of the Red Army to have been taken prisoner by the Germans was almost a death sentence in itself. Not only did he risk ill-treatment at the hands of his captors, especially the Waffen-SS (many Commissars being shot out of hand as a matter of policy), but he almost certainly faced subsequent death as a prisoner from starvation or unchecked sickness, over work as a slave labourer or by murder as a deliberate policy of extermination. Even if the poor wretch managed to survive all these hazards the very act of being 'liberated' from prison camps by his own people often meant that he was killed off by the NKVD as having been 'tainted' through contact with the Germans or Italians as a prisoner of war. Two Red Army officers have here been captured in what appears to have been a surprise move on the part of German troops: the lorry in which these Russians were travelling has seemingly driven into a newly occupied village.
61. Russian prisoners being escorted towards the rear by German Jäger troops.
62. Red Army prisoners are brought into German Mountain Troop lines under armed escort. The use of a corduroy pathway – constructed from short cut lengths of tree branches – indicates a fairly static area, possibly the head-quarters of this particular Gebirgsjäger Regiment, which in turn indicates that these prisoners are to be interrogated in detail.

63. The German forces possessed excellent medical services: it was always considered essential that the sick and wounded receive immediate medical attention and when necessary be evacuated to rear area field hospitals. Here, stretcher parties carry off wounded soldiers.
64. Medical instruments and equipment being carried by mules from a medical company of a Mountain Troop Regiment.
65. Dental care was an important aspect of the front-line soldier's medical health, and motorized dental surgeries were employed to visit troops in need.

63▲

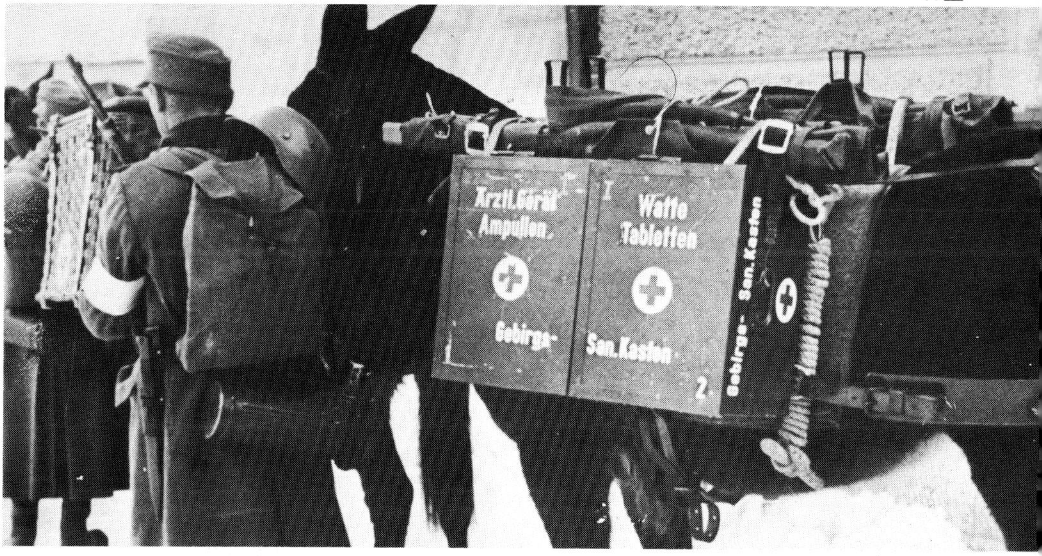

64▲ 65▼

▲66 ▼67

68▲

66. German soldiers from a variety of units take their leave of a nurse; all were wounded to some degree and all have received hospital treatment. When their wounds and operations had healed sufficiently, soldiers were allowed out from the hospital on short periods of leave, eventually being discharged to return to their units.
67. Military decorations and awards played an important role in helping to keep up the morale of the German fighting man. Infantry Grenadiers are shown being presented with the silver and the bronze versions of the 'Close Combat Clasp'. The award was instituted on 25 November 1942 to reward those officers and men of the German Army who had exemplified themselves during hand-to-hand combat, unsupported by armour, for a specified number of days. The Clasp was struck in three grades, bronze for 15 days of close combat, silver for 30 days and gold for 50 days. When awarded, the 'Nahkampfspange' was worn over the left breast pocket, above any medal ribbon bar that was present.
68. German troops were occasionally awarded foreign decorations, either by other Axis powers or by those nations that collaborated with the Axis forces. The photograph shows Marshal Antonescu presenting Rumanian medals to German soldiers serving on the Eastern Front.
69. Generalfeldmarschall von Reichenau, Commander of an Army Group, studies maps at a meeting held at the Führer's Headquarters, 6 August 1941. Von Reichenau is dressed in the version of the Field Service uniform worn by Army Field Marshals and Generals and carries an interimstab or cane. This cane, shown here stuck into the soil, was carried on occasions which did not call for the use of the Field Marshal's baton.

◀69

▲70

70. General of Mountain Troops Dietl, visiting soldiers on the Eismeer Front, is greeted by Divisional officers. General Dietl (right) is wearing a specially produced, extra long greatcoat with fur lining and fur collar. The officer shaking his hand wears an animal skin coat with fleece lining, whilst the two junior officers are wearing standard issue Army greatcoats.

71. Not until the autumn of 1942 did purpose-made winter clothing begin to be distributed to German troops. The reversible winter uniform, worn here with the white side showing, consisted of padded trousers and a padded jacket with an attached hood. These two garments were usually worn with other cold weather items such as woollen gloves, a sweater, the woollen toque (a form of knitted or cloth sleeve similar to a balaclava helmet) and some form of cloth head-dress. Thick woollen socks and special cold weather boots completed the outfit.

72. Soldiers engaged in activities such as sentry duty and truck driving or as motorcyclists required extra thick protective clothing in order to survive the sub-zero winter conditions on the Eastern Front. This motorcylist is wearing cold-weather clothing consisting of an air force fleece-lined flying suit and a Wehrmacht-issue gas mask minus its filter canister which afforded some protection to his face.

73. The camouflaged side of the reversible winter uniform: two assault pioneers from Infantry Division 'Grossdeutschland'.

74. Winter-clad infantry ride into battle. Although the winter uniform was designed to be worn over the leather equipment it was common practice for troops to wear the equipment over the reversible jackets.

75. Extra thick, heavy duty, blanket-lined greatcoats were issued to individual soldiers undertaking static guard duty. These coats, an example of which is worn by the machine gunner on the left, had cloth hoods attached.

71▶

72▲ 73▼

74▲ 75▼

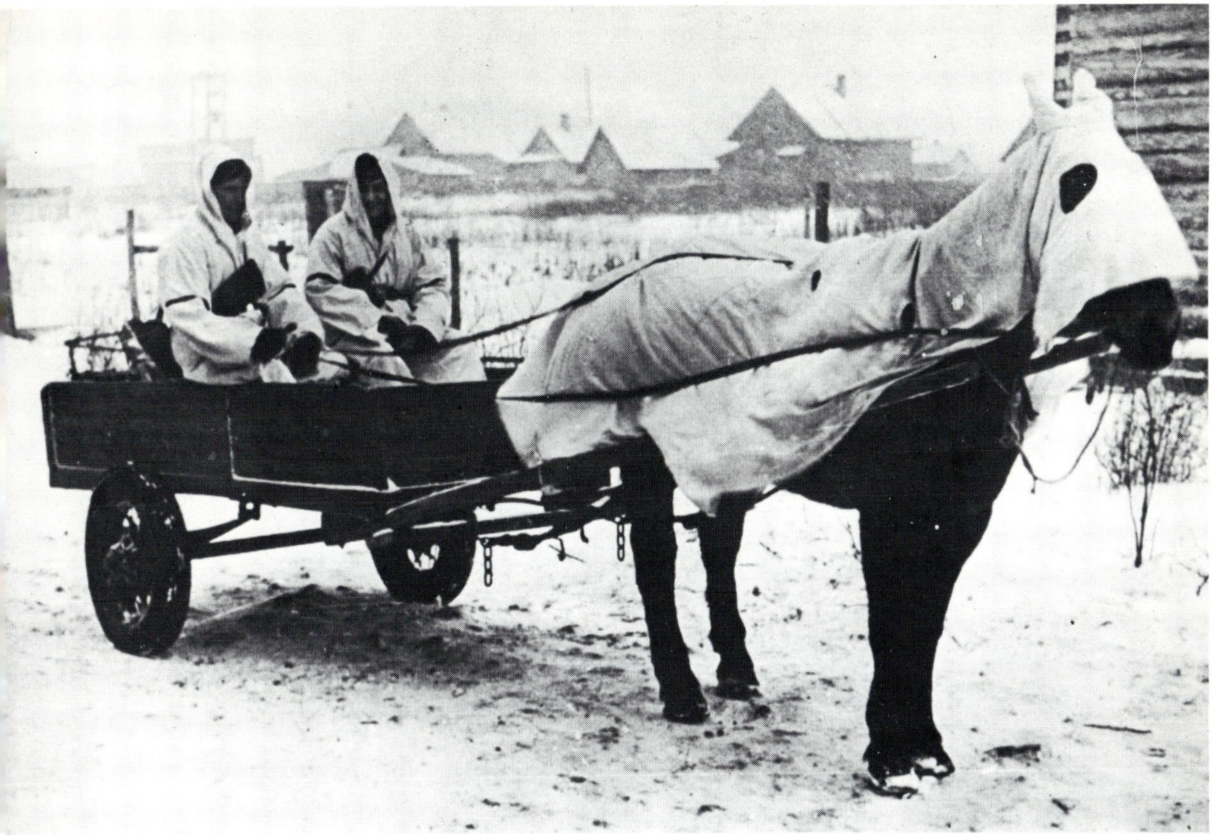

◀76

77▲

76. The strain of combat along the Eastern Front during the harshness of the Russian winters is captured by the camera. It was essential that extra layers of clothing be worn under the heavy, padded winter uniform, but these added weight, and when the clothing became wet (through the action of melting snow or of body sweat) both the inner and outer garments became even more uncomfortable.
77. Snow camouflage was even extended to animals.
78. White-clad, winter-uniformed Infantry accompany snow-camouflaged tanks.

78▼

79. Despite the thin winter sunshine, the temperature encountered on the Eastern Front was usually many degrees below freezing point. Here, winter-clad troops lead Panji ponies.
80. German Grenadiers exhausted by severe cold and by their own physical effort: both men, who are seated on petrol cans with their backs to the wind, appear almost incapable of movement. The chill factor created by the driving wind was capable of penetrating even the warmest clothing.
81. A section leader and his runner observe enemy positions through field glasses. Both men are wearing white coveralls and white cloth helmet covers.
82. German Infantry, many of whom are wearing white snow camouflage clothing (both uniforms and coveralls), make their way across open ground.

▲79 ▼80

81▲ 82▼

▲83

83. An assault troop leader from Infantry Division 'Grossdeutschland'.

▲84

84. A tank commander, an obvious veteran of many campaigns. The death's head collar patches which were a feature of the special black Panzer uniform were piped in pink, the arm-of-service colour allocated to this branch of the German Army. The same colour piping was also used around the collars of prewar Panzer uniforms but this was discontinued during the war in order to save on manufacturing costs. The special black tunic was correctly worn with a grey shirt an black tie; the wearing of a woollen, roll-necked sweater was tolerated but only during active service in cold weather.

85. Anxiously looking skywards, Panzer-Grenadiers hold up a swastika flag as an aerial recognition signal, marking their presence i this Russian town.

▼85

86▲

86. Siege guns could sometimes be brought into position to help attacking forces to destroy fixed enemy positions, the Crimean city of Sebastopol being a prime example. Because of their size and firepower they could be positioned well outside the range of retaliatory enemy artillery fire, and properly maintained and adequately defended railway track proved a most convenient means of moving such heavy weapons from place to place. Here, gunners from an 88mm anti-aircraft flak unit run towards their railborne artillery piece at the sound of the alarm.

87. German railway pioneers take up defensive positions alongside a section of railway track.

87▼

▲88 ▼89 ▼90

;8. It was important to naintain and guard vital ailway track, but it was ust as imperative to deny his facility to an dvancing enemy. ;erman combat ngineers here prepare xplosive charges in eadiness for blowing a ection of track.

;9. The German ground orces made extensive ise of radio elecommunications but his system was upplemented at almost ll levels of command by he use of field telephone ontact. When it was not ossible for them to be trung on poles, field elephone lines were laid cross open ground by neans of a simple ortable drum device. This item, illustrated in he photograph, was vound with telephone able and could be arried on a soldier's ack: the cable was paid ut behind him as he noved forward and once he linesman had reached is objective the line was onnected to a field elephone handset.

0. Signallers wearing vinter uniform man a ortable field wireless et. Less susceptible to hysical interference, adio transmission was evertheless liable to nterception by the nemy and could often rove a security risk.

1. An officer from a Signals Regiment checks ut field telephone lines onverging towards a eadquarters.

91▶

▲92

92. An observer from Panzer-Grenadier-Division 'Grossdeutschland' using a field telephone.
93, 94. A contrast in head-dress: a straw sun hat worn by an anti-aircraft lookout somewhere in North Africa and a fine net headscarf worn as protection against gnats and other flying insects by a soldier serving in Southern Russia.
95. In a scene reminiscent of the First World War, a runner splashes his way along a water-filled trench to take a message to his Company Commander, June 1943.

▼93

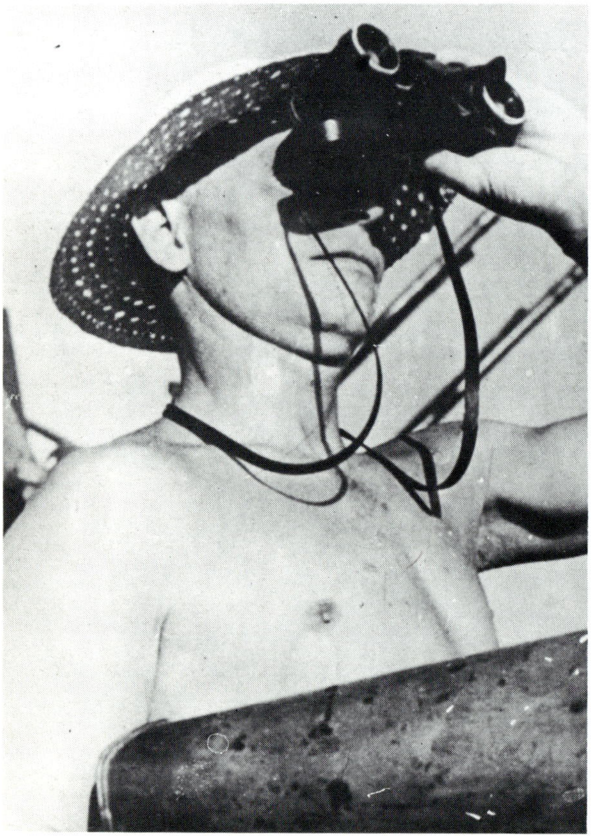

▼94

95▶

96. Grubby, unshaven and heavily clad against the cold weather, German infantry occupy a trench system built as part of the offensive fortified ring around the southern area of Lake Ladoga, near Leningrad.
97. Generaloberst Lindemann making a tour of inspection of the defensive positions constructed in the area of Lake Ladoga, November 1943. The corduroy pathway gave a firm footing to the bottom of trenches, paths made from these purpose-cut lengths of tree branches also being used over swampy, muddy or soft ground.

◀**96**

97▼

98. Seated in a small niche dug into the side of a trench and covered against rain by a camouflage shelter quarter (Zeltbahn), a Grenadier eats his rations during a lull in the fighting.
99. A well-equipped German observation post somewhere on the Russian Front. The winter sunshine belies the fact that the earth is frozen rock-hard.
100. Heavy timber, whitewashed on the outside as snow camouflage, has been used to construct this machine gun post somewhere in the Balkans.

▼**98**

99▲ 100▼

▲101

101. Somewhere on the Eastern Front, welcome hot food is ladled out of a canister into the mess tins of troops detailed off to collect the day's meal.
102. Such was the speed of the initial blitzkrieg wrought by the Germans on the Russian Army during the opening months of 'Barbarossa' that very often the only way the German Infantry could keep up with their advancing tanks was for the soldiers to ride on them. Infantry transported as shown in this apparently posed photograph were available to deal with any enemy anti-tank emplacements or machine gun positions but they were also vulnerable to artillery or mortar attack – when caught by a surprise 'stonk' of mortars, for example, or by fire from concealed machine guns, they could sustain heavy losses. The practice of moving troops in this manner was, except where conditions were considered relatively safe, generally phased out, especially with the introduction of armoured personnel carriers.
103. German troops ride a tank somewhere on the Eastern Front.

▼102

103▶

▲104 ▼105

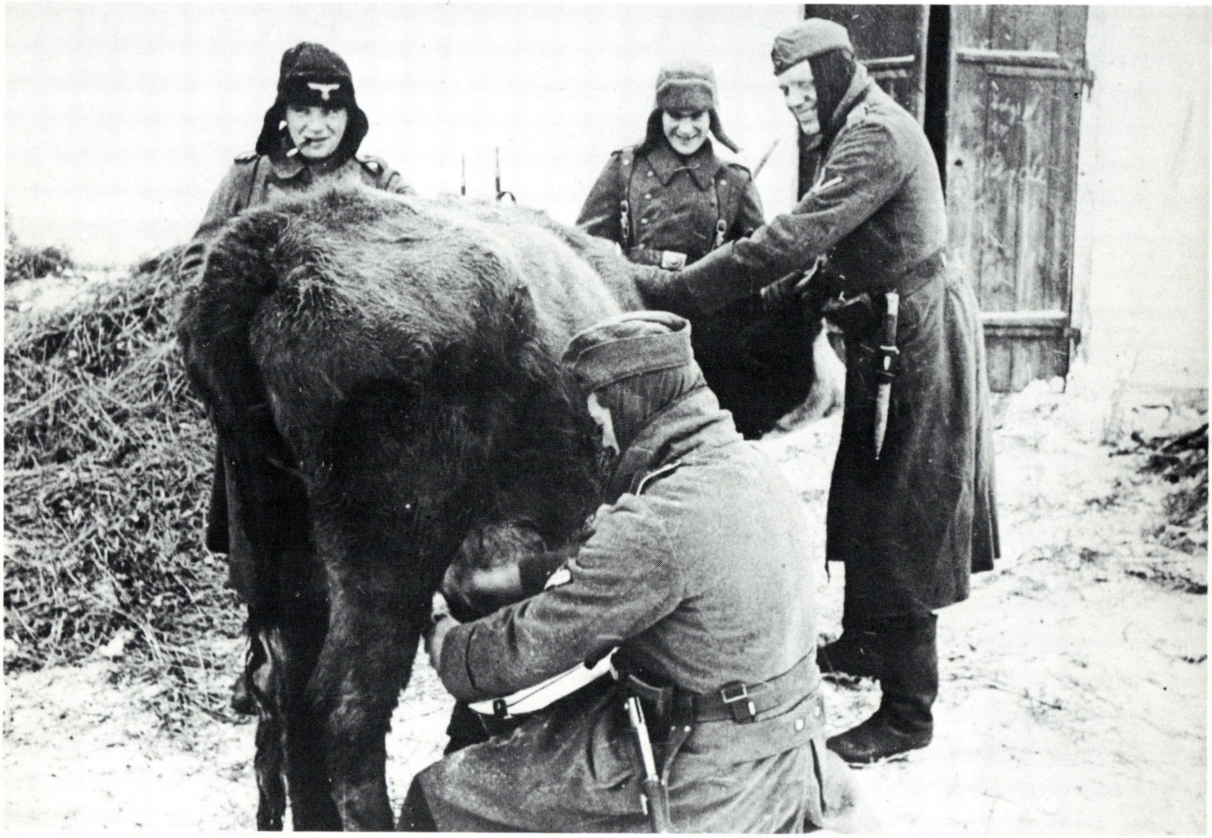

104. Panzer-Grenadiers (Armoured Infantry) being transported by armoured personnel carriers.
105. The pressure of both offensive and defensive action and the constant need for front-line vigilance meant that any periods of military inactivity, when the troops could relax, were important in themselves and also afforded an opportunity for other pursuits. Even such a simple and commonplace commodity as fresh milk became a luxury for front-line troops. Here, German troops, some wearing fur caps, hold firm a Russian cow while one of their number milks the animal into a bucket.
106. Soldiers clean the barrel of an Assault Artillery piece.

106▼

107. The cleaning of weapons and personal equipment was not only necessary but also therapeutic. Men from an Infantry company are shown cleaning their rifles.
108. The Zeltbahn, the German-issue shelter quarter, could be used both as a rain cape and as a simple form of tent. Here, two young crew members of a self-propelled assault gun relax inside the entrance to a tent made by buttoning together four separate shelter quarters.
109. A joke is shared among these troops, but one of their number still keeps a wary eye on enemy positions.

◀107 108▲ 109▼

▲110 ▼111

112▲

110. Panji wagons and Panji sleighs pulled by sturdy little ponies were used extensively by almost all the German ground forces serving on the Eastern Front. They provided a vital if crude form of transport which supplemented horse-drawn transport as well as wheeled and tracked vehicles. During the long winter months the Panji ponies and their sleighs were very often the only means of moving troops and stores, and without them many front-line and supporting units would have been immobilized. The photograph shows a Panji wagon complete with peasant driver and German escort on its way to collect field post.
111. A column of Panji sleighs and ponies awaits the order to move off.
112. Animals were of course far more vulnerable to gunfire and explosions than mechanical vehicles, and horses, ponies and mules were killed in large numbers in all theatres of war, many more being rendered unserviceable on account of wounds or sickness and having to be treated and nursed back to full health by the German veterinary service. The illustration depicts a horse-drawn ammunition limber that was destroyed by artillery fire with the loss of at least eight animals.

▲113

113. Load-carrying mules somewhere in Greece.

114. A horse-drawn column of Hungarian and German artillery on its way to the front passes the remains of a knocked-out Russian artillery piece and limber.

▼114